Animals
HIDDEN
in the
SNOW

Jessica Rusick

PEBBLE
a capstone imprint

Published by Capstone Press, an imprint of Capstone
1710 Roe Crest Drive
North Mankato, Minnesota 56003
capstonepub.com

Library of Congress Cataloging-in-Publication Data
Names: Rusick, Jessica, author.
Title: Animals hidden in the snow / Jessica Rusick.
Description: North Mankato, Minnesota : Pebble, [2022] | Series: Animals undercover | Audience: Ages 5-8 | Audience: Grades K-1 |
Summary: "Some creatures are masters of disguise! They use camouflage and cover to outsmart predators or sneak up on prey. In cold habitats, animals blend in with the snowy surroundings. They also hide beneath the snow in dens. Can you spot the creatures hidden in the snow?"-- Provided by publisher.
Identifiers: LCCN 2021041469 (print) | LCCN 2021041470 (ebook) |
  ISBN 9781666315356 (hardcover) | ISBN 9781666328301 (paperback) |
  ISBN 9781666315363 (pdf) | ISBN 9781666315387 (kindle edition)
Subjects: LCSH: Animals--Polar animals--Juvenile literature. | Camouflage (Biology)--Juvenile literature.
Classification: LCC QL104 .R87 2022 (print) | LCC QL104 (ebook) | DDC 591.70911/3--dc23
LC record available at https://lccn.loc.gov/2021041469
LC ebook record available at https://lccn.loc.gov/2021041470

Image Credits
iStockphoto: jimkruger, Cover, mlharing, 11, Mumemories, 21, skhoward, 27, VisualCommunications, 23; Shutterstock: Andrei Stepanov, 24, 32 (top), BILD LLC, 3 (bottom right), 17, Brent R. Keeney, 18, C. Hamilton, 13, COULANGES, 8, 31 (top), critterbiz, 6, Danita Delimont, 5, Fiona M. Donnelly, 3 (bottom middle), 14, Gillian Santink, 19, Jim Cumming, 20, 26, 31 (bottom), 32 (middle), Jukka Jantunen, 1, 22, 28, knelson20, 29, Matt Gerlach, 12, 31 (middle), Miks Mihails Ignats, 7, NaturesMomentsuk, 15, PICARD Gweg, 3 (bottom left), 16, Sergey Uryadnikov, 9, shivaram subramaniam, 25, Sophia Granchinho, 30, 32 (bottom), Vaclav Sebek, 3 (top), 10

Design Elements
Mighty Media, Inc.

Editorial and Design Credits
Editor: Rebecca Felix, Mighty Media; Designer: Aruna Rangarajan, Mighty Media

HIDDEN IN THE
SNOW

Some creatures living in snowy habitats are masters of disguise! They use camouflage and cover to outsmart predators or sneak up on prey. Some animals blend in with snow or hide beneath it. Can you spot the creatures hidden in the snow?

First, try to spot the animal
hidden in the snow.
WHAT DO YOU THINK IT IS?

Turn the page to reveal the
animal and learn more about it.
DID YOU GUESS RIGHT?

This hooved mammal has a black nose. What is it?

Turn and see!

IT'S A WHITE-TAILED DEER!

White-tailed deer have reddish fur in summer. It turns grayish brown in winter. The deer's fur helps it blend in with trees.

This fluffy pup will soon become a strong swimmer. What is it?

Turn and see!

IT'S A HARP SEAL!

Baby harp seals have white fur. They blend in with snow and ice. This keeps the seals safe from predators. A harp seal's fur turns gray as it gets older.

This furry animal has thick, curved claws. What is it?

Turn and see!

IT'S A POLAR BEAR!

Mother polar bears dig dens in the snow. They have babies there. The mother and babies stay in the den all winter. They come out in spring.

This large mammal has shaggy fur. What is it?

Turn and see!

IT'S A BISON!

Bison grow extra-thick fur in winter. It keeps body heat from escaping. So, snow that lands on bison doesn't melt! This causes bison to blend in with snowy surroundings.

This striped rodent eats nuts and seeds. What is it?

Turn and see!

IT'S AN EASTERN CHIPMUNK!

Chipmunks make dens in hollow trees or underground. The animals sleep for much of winter. Chipmunks wake up every few days to eat, pee, and poop!

This fuzzy mammal has a bushy tail. What is it?

Turn and see!

IT'S AN ARCTIC FOX!

Arctic foxes sometimes sleep in snowy dens. They also sleep out in the open. A fox curls its tail around its nose when it sleeps. This helps keep the fox warm.

This horned creature lives in the mountains. What is it?

Turn and see!

IT'S A DALL SHEEP!

Dall sheep have long winter fur. The fur can be more than 2 inches (5 centimeters) thick! It protects the sheep from the cold. It also helps the sheep blend in with the snow.

This big bird has bright yellow eyes. What is it?

Turn and see!

IT'S A SNOWY OWL!

Snowy owls have great hearing. The owls can hear prey hiding under the snow! Snowy owls mostly eat mouselike animals called lemmings.

This red rodent has sharp claws. What is it?

Turn and see!

IT'S A RED SQUIRREL!

Red squirrels gather nuts and pinecones. They bury this food underground. In winter, the squirrels return to the food piles. They dig snow tunnels to reach the food!

This mammal has big, furry back feet. What is it?

Turn and see!

IT'S AN ARCTIC HARE!

Arctic hares have thick white fur. It helps them hide in snow from predators. Arctic hares can also outrun predators. They can move at 37 miles (60 kilometers) per hour!

This spotted cat has a long tail. What is it?

Turn and see!

IT'S A SNOW LEOPARD!

Snow leopards live in snowy mountains. Their fur blends in with rocks. Snow leopards have large, furry feet. This helps them walk in the snow.

This long-bodied animal is in the weasel family. What is it?

Turn and see!

IT'S AN ERMINE!

Ermines have white fur in winter. This hides them in the snow, helping them sneak up on prey. Ermines bite prey with their sharp teeth.

This round bird has white feathers in winter. What is it?

Turn and see!

IT'S A WILLOW PTARMIGAN!

Willow ptarmigans dig burrows under the snow to stay warm. They also have feathered feet. This helps them walk over snow.

FUN FACTS

Harp seals can grow to be 6 feet (2 meters) long.

Bison can weigh up to 2,000 pounds (907 kilograms)!

Snowy owls become whiter as they age.

An Arctic hare has flat back feet. They keep the hare from sinking into snow.

Snow leopards can travel 25 miles (40 km) in one night.

One flock of willow ptarmigans can have as many as 2,200 birds!